CW00848171

Japanese Cookbook

Stay-At-Home Japanese Recipes Everyone Can Make

Copyright © 2020

All rights reserved.

DEDICATION

Contents

Rice (Japanese Short Grain Rice)

Classic Fried Rice

Prep Time 5 mins

Cook Time 10 mins

Total Time 15 mins

This classic Fried Rice recipe with ham, egg, and green onion is a delicious one-pan meal that you can whip up under 20 minutes. It's bursting with flavor and perfect for a weeknight meal.

Servings: 1

INGREDIENTS

2 rice bowls cooked Japanese short-grain rice (Ideally a day old, See blog post)

2 slices ham

1 green onion/scallion

1 large egg

2 Tbsp neutral-flavored oil (vegetable, canola, etc) (divided)

½ tsp kosher/sea salt (I use Diamond Crystal; Use half for table salt) (¼ tsp if using table salt)

white pepper powder (a must have for my fried rice!)

2 tsp soy sauce (I use Kikkoman® Gluten Free Tamari Soy Sauce)

INSTRUCTIONS

Preparation

1. Gather all the ingredients.

2. To prepare steamed rice, microwave your one-day-old rice that's kept in the refrigerator until room temperature or warm. If you do not have one-day-old rice, then you can cook the rice, spread it out on a baking sheet lined with parchment paper, and leave it out on the counter without cover for 1-2 hours. This will remove moisture in the rice.

3. Cut the white part of the green onion into rounds and the green part diagonally, dividing the white and green parts.

4. Cut the ham into ¼ inch square pieces.

5. Crack and whisk the egg in a bowl.

Cooking

1. Make sure all the ingredients are ready to go. Heat the wok (or the large frying pan) on medium high heat. Once it's hot, add 1 Tbsp oil and swirl around to make sure all sides of the work (frying pan) are coated with oil. Add the beaten egg and mix around so that fluffy egg will be created.

2. While some parts of the egg are still a little bit runny (not all the way cooked), transfer to a plate. We do not want to overcook the egg at this stage.

3. Add 1 Tbsp oil and start cooking ham and white parts of the chopped green onion. Stir fry and coat well with oil.

4. Add the room temp/warm rice into the wok (frying pan). Separate the rice with a spatula, without damaging the rice. Don't make it mushy by pressing down, but fluff out the rice so it is coated with oil and gets nice wok char.

5. Add the cooked egg back in the wok and break into smaller pieces while you combine with the rice. If some of the rice sticks to the wok, don't worry (it happens when the oil was not enough) as you can scrape it off easily and creates nice char taste).

6. Season with salt and white pepper. You can add more later after adding soy sauce, if not enough.

7. Add the soy sauce. The key action here is to toss the fried rice in the wok and make it fluffy instead of a big mess of fried rice sitting at the bottom of the wok.

8. Add green parts of the chopped green onion. And after tossing a few more times, transfer to a plate.

9. Fried rice at Chinese restaurants in Japan is often served in a dome shape. If you like to serve it this way, fill the fried rice in a rice bowl, pat down lightly to compact and invert onto a plate.

10. Sprinkle green onion on top, and serve!

Zosui (Japanese Rice Soup)

Prep Time 10 mins

Cook Time 20 mins

Zosui is a comforting Japanese rice soup cooked in a savory dashi broth with vegetables, eggs, mushrooms, and sometimes meat or seafood. It's a nourishing meal that helps refuel your energy. With pantry ready ingredients, you can easily make it in no time!

5

Servings: 2

INGREDIENTS

For Broth

3 cups dashi (I use 3 cups water + 1 dashi packet)

2 tsp soy sauce (I used Usukuchi (Light Color Soy Sauce))

½ tsp kosher/sea salt (I use Diamond Crystal; Use half for table salt)

For Zosui

6 oz boneless skinless chicken thighs (170 g, 6 oz)

1 inch carrot (40 g, 1.4 oz)

2 shiitake mushrooms (80 g, 2.8 oz)

2 green onions/scallions

1 ½ rice bowls cooked Japanese short-grain rice (200 g, 7 oz; 1 Rice Cooker Cup (180 ml / 150 g) yields 330 g of cooked rice, which is about 2 bowls of rice (150 g per bowl))

1 large egg

½ tsp toasted white sesame seeds

⅛ tsp white pepper powder

INSTRUCTIONS

Gather all the ingredients.

To Prepare the Dashi

1. In a large pot (I used a donabe), add dashi broth. If you are making dashi from scratch, here's the direction (https://www.justonecookbook.com/how-to-make-dashi/). In this recipe, I show you how to make dashi using a dashi packet. Add water and a dashi packet in the donabe.

2. Cover the lid and slowly bring water to boil on low heat. After a few minutes, open the lid and shake the bag to release more flavors.

3. Close the lid and continue to heat the broth. Once boiling, cook for 3 minutes and discard the dashi packet. Keep the lid closed and set aside.

To Prepare the Ingredients

1. Remove the excess fat from the chicken and cut it into small bite-sized pieces.

2. Discard the tough stem of shiitake mushrooms and thinly slice the caps.

3. Cut the carrot into quarters lengthwise and thinly slice them.

4. Cut the green onions into thin pieces and put them in a small bowl. We use them as a garnish at the end.

5. If you're using cold cooked rice, put it in a fine-mesh sieve and rinse the rice under running water to remove excess starch. Shake and drain well. If you're using freshly made rice, you can skip this process.

To Cook Zosui

1. In a hot dashi broth, add the chicken.

2. Close the lid and bring it to boil on medium-low heat. Once boiling, skim the scum and foam on the surface.

3. Add the carrot and cook covered until tender, about 4-5 minutes.

4. Once the carrot is tender, add soy sauce and salt to the broth.

5. Add the shiitake mushrooms and well-drained cooked rice. Cover to cook for 10 minutes.

6. Beat the egg in a bowl.

7. Slowly drizzle a small amount of the beaten egg over the soup surface, which will create a fluffy texture.

8. Add some of the green onion and sesame seeds. Sprinkle white pepper powder at the end.

9. Cover with the lid and bring the pot to the table to serve into individual bowls.

Yaki Onigiri (Grilled Rice Ball)

Prep Time 15 mins

Cook Time 15 mins

Total Time 30 mins

A favorite at Izakaya restaurants, Yaki Onigiri are Japanese grilled rice balls covered in savory soy sauce. With a crispy crust on the outside and soft sticky rice on the inside, these rice balls are simply irresistible and easy to make at home!

9

Servings: 6 grilled rice balls

INGREDIENTS

2 rice cooker cups uncooked Japanese short-grain rice (360ml; 1 rice cooker cup (180ml) of uncooked rice will make 3 rice balls.)

Water

kosher/sea salt (I use Diamond Crystal; Use half for table salt)

neutral-flavored oil (vegetable, canola, etc)

soy sauce (I used homemade Unagi Sauce, see Notes for recipe)

INSTRUCTIONS

1. Gather all the ingredients. Cook the rice in the rice cooker, pot over the stove top or pressure cooker.
2. Let the cooked rice cool a little bit until you can hold rice without burning your hands. Do not let the rice completely cool down.
3. Make Onigiri into triangle shapes. First wet both of your hands with water so rice won't stick.
4. Then put some salt in your hands and rub to spread all around.
5. Scoop about a half cup of rice onto your palm.
6. Cover the rice with the other hand and gently form the rice into a triangle.

7. Make sure covering hand (my right hand) should be forming a triangle shape. When forming the onigiri shape, your hands should be just firm enough so the onigiri doesn't fall apart. You don't want to squeeze the rice too tight.

8. I use three fingers (thumb, index finger, middle finger) to cover the area to make a nice triangle shape. Then rotate onigiri to make a perfect triangle.

9. While you squeeze onigiri firmly with both hands, one of your hand (my left hand) has to press onigiri to keep a nice form. Left photo is before squeezing and right photo is after.

10. Gently squeeze the center of triangle on both sides so there is a slight indentation (for grilling onigiri). Now onigiri is ready! You can tell I'm not a good onigiri maker – no matter how many years I have been practicing.

11. Lightly oil a cast iron skillet and put it on medium heat.

12. Grill onigiri until all sides are crispy and lightly browned. Don't turn it around. Just work on one side at a time and avoid turning over frequently.

13. Lower heat to medium low and brush all sides with soy sauce (unagi sauce). Rotate to make sure all sides become crispy. Be careful not to burn onigiri after you brush it with the sauce.

Udon Noodles

Kitsune Udon

Prep Time 10 mins

Cook Time 10 mins

Total Time 50 mins

Kitsune Udon is a Japanese noodle soup in dashi broth, topped with seasoned fried tofu, pink-swirl narutomaki fish cake, and scallions. This hearty udon soup is one of the most popular, classic Japanese noodle dishes.

Servings: 2

INGREDIENTS

For Noodle Soup Broth

2 ¼ cups dashi (Homemade ingredients below; or 2 ¼ cup water + 1 to 1 ¼ tsp dashi powder)

1 Tbsp mirin

1 tsp sugar

1 Tbsp usukuchi (light-color) soy sauce (or regular soy sauce; we use light color soy sauce here so the soup doesn't become too dark)

½ tsp kosher/sea salt (I use Diamond Crystal; Use half for table salt)

For Homemade Dashi

2 ½ cups water

1 kombu (dried kelp) (2" x 5", 5 cm x 12 cm)

1 ½ cups katsuobushi (dried bonito flakes) (15 g, 0.5 oz: skip for

vegetarian/vegan)

For Kitsune Udon

2 servings udon noodles (180 g dry udon noodles; 500 g frozen/boiled udon noodles)

4 Inari Age (seasoned fried tofu pouch) (You can buy canned or refrigerated inariage package; Homemade inariage recipe, click here.)

1 green onion/scallion

Narutomaki (fish cakes) (optional; skip for vegetarian/vegan)

Shichimi Togarashi (Japanese Seven Spice) (optional; sprinkle at the table)

INSTRUCTIONS

Gather all the ingredients. Before we start: It's really important to have good flavorful dashi for this recipe. Although you can take the shortcut by using dashi powder or dashi packet, I encourage you to make your own dashi because the broth tastes so much better! It only takes less than 30 minutes to make. For vegetarian/vegan, please use Kombu Dashi.

To Make Homemade Dashi (Please skip if you already have dashi)

1. Put the kombu and 2 ½ cup water in a measuring cup for at least 30 minutes. If you have time, soak for 3 hours or up to half a day. Kombu's flavor comes out naturally from soaking in water. If you don't have time at all, skip soaking.

2. Transfer kombu and water to a saucepan. Slowly bring to a boil over medium-low heat.

3. Just before boiling (you will see bubbles around the edges of the pan), remove the kombu. If you leave the kombu inside, the dashi will become slimy and bitter. Now this broth is Kombu Dashi (vegetarian/vegan) and it's ready to make udon soup. For non-vegetarian/vegan, add 1 ½ cups katsuobushi and bring it to a boil again.

4. Once the dashi is boiling, reduce the heat, simmer for just 15 seconds, and turn off the heat. Let the katsuobushi sink to the bottom, about 10-15 minutes. Strain the dashi through a fine-mesh sieve set over a saucepan. Now you have roughly 2 ¼ cup dashi.

To Make Udon Soup

1. In a saucepan, add the dashi, 1 Tbsp mirin, 1 tsp sugar, 1 Tbsp soy sauce, and ½ tsp kosher salt and bring to boil. Once boiling, turn off the heat or cover and keep on a low simmer.

To Prepare Toppings

1. Squeeze excess liquid from the inariage (or you can keep it as it is). Cut the green onion into thin slices. Slice the Narutomaki fish cake into 1/8 inch (3 mm).

To Prepare Udon Noodles

1. Bring a large pot of water to boil for udon noodles. My favorite udon is the frozen Sanuki Udon. Cook the frozen udon noodles in boiling water for 1 minute (no need to defrost). If you use dry noodles, follow the package instructions.

2. Pick up the noodles in a strainer or drain the hot water. Make sure to remove excess water (which will end up diluting your soup).

To Assemble

1. Serve udon noodles and hot soup in serving bowls and top with inariage, narutomaki, green onion and sprinkles of shichimi togarashi.

Curry Udon

Prep Time 10 mins

Cook Time 40 mins

Total Time 50 mins

Thick chewy udon noodles soaked in a rich, fragrant curry sauce! This Curry Udon will satisfy your noodles craving in an instant. Bonus: it's simple enough to throw together on a busy weeknight.

Servings: 2

INGREDIENTS

½ onion (5.7 oz or 162 g)

2 green onions/scallions (finely chopped)

1 Tbsp neutral-flavored oil (vegetable, canola, etc)

6 oz thinly sliced pork loin (170 g; Or use your choice of protein; cut into small pieces)

1 Tbsp sake

3 cups dashi (720 ml)

2 cubes Japanese curry roux (Roughly 2 oz or 50 g total. You can make homemade Japanese curry roux.)

2 tsp soy sauce

2 servings udon noodles (6.3 oz/180 g dry udon noodles; 1.1 lb/500 g frozen/boiled udon noodles)

INSTRUCTIONS

2. Gather all the ingredients. For curry roux, you will need to break into cubes and use 2 pieces. Prepare dashi with your preferred method, if you haven't made yet.

3. Thinly slice the onion and green onions.

4. In a medium pot (I used a 2.75 QT Staub), heat oil on medium

heat and add the onion.

5. Saute the onion for 2-3 minutes, and then add the meat.

6. Cook the meat until almost no longer pink and add sake.

7. Add dashi and cover with the lid. Reduce the heat to medium-low and cook for 5 minutes.

8. When simmering, skim off the scum and fat from the stock and continue to cook.

9. Meanwhile, start boiling a large pot of water for udon.

10.   After 5 minutes, turn off the heat. Put the cube of the curry roux in a ladle, letting dissolve one cube at a time (We'll use 2 cubes total).

11.   With chopsticks or spoon, let the roux dissolves completely in a ladle, before releasing it to the soup. Tip: You don't want to eat a chunk of undissolved curry roux, so take your time to dissolve the roux completely.

12.   Add soy sauce and mix well. Turn off the heat and cover the lid to keep it warm.

13.   When water is boiling, cook your udon noodles according to the package instruction (For this Sanuki Udon, cook frozen noodles in boiling water for 1 minute).

14.   Drain the noodles and divide into two bowls. Pour the curry over the udon noodles. Top with green onion and serve immediately.

Miso Nikomi Udon

Prep Time 15 mins

Cook Time 25 mins

Total Time 40 mins

Miso Nikomi Udon is a hearty and comforting noodle soup where chicken, fish cake, and udon noodles are simmered in a miso-flavored dashi broth. When it's cold outside, this noodle soup will warm you inside out.

Servings: 2

INGREDIENTS

3 cups dashi (720 ml)

½ package shimeji mushrooms (1.8 oz/50 g)

4 shiitake mushrooms (2.3 oz/65 g)

⅓ kamaboko (fish cake)

1 Negi (long green onion) (4 oz/113 g) (Or use 2 green onions)

1 piece aburaage (deep-fried tofu pouch) (today I used 2 small aburaage)

2 servings udon noodles (6.3 oz/180 g dry udon noodles; 1.1 lb/500 g frozen/boiled udon noodles)

1 chicken thighs (7 oz/200 g)

2 large eggs

Shichimi Togarashi (Japanese seven spice) (for sprinkling)

Seasonings

4 Tbsp miso (I used Hikari Miso® Organic Red Miso)

3 Tbsp mirin

INSTRUCTIONS

Gather all the ingredients.

Make Dashi

1. Make 3 cups dashi using one of 3 Ways to Make Dashi. Here I used the convenient dashi packet method. If you're vegetarian/vegan, use Kombu Dashi.
2. Prepare Ingredients
3. Cut the end of shimeji mushrooms and separate into smaller chunks.
4. Cut the stem of shiitake mushrooms and cut in halves. I use "Sogigiri" cutting technique to increase the surface.
5. If you like, you can make a decorative cut on the shiitake mushrooms.
6. Cut Kamaboko fish cake into 4 slices.
7. Cut the Negi (long green onion) diagonally, and separate white and green parts (we will add them to the pot at different times).
8. Pour hot water over aburaage to get rid of the factory oil. Some people skip the step as the oil used is cleaner these days. I do it anyway to get rid of excess oil. [Optional] Cut into smaller pieces. I cut into triangles.

9. Cut the chicken into smaller bite-size pieces. I use "Sogigiri" technique to create a bigger surface of the chicken so it will cook faster and absorb more flavors.

10. Bring a pot of water to a boil. Add the frozen udon noodles and loosen it with chopsticks. As soon as they are loosened (30 seconds or so), drain the udon noodles into a colander and set aside. If you use dry noodles, follow the package instructions.

11. Crack eggs into a small bowl (so you won't accidentally drop an egg shell into the pot) and make sure all ingredients are now ready to go!

Cook Miso Nikomi Udon

1. In a large pot (or donabe), add 3 cups dashi, chicken, and white part of negi.

2. Cover to cook on medium heat for 10 minutes, or until the outside of the chicken is no longer pink (inside can be still pink at this stage). When boiling, turn the heat down to simmer. Skim off the fat and scum with a fine mesh skimmer.

3. Add 3 Tbsp mirin and 3 Tbsp miso (keep 1 Tbsp for later. Why? Read my post.). I use a Miso Muddler and it works wonderfully to make sure miso is dissolved completely. You should place miso in a ladle and use chopsticks to let miso

23

dissolve inside the ladle before releasing it into the dashi. That way you can make sure there are no miso chunks left at the bottom of the pot.

4. Add udon noodles, aburaage, shimeji mushrooms, shiitake mushrooms, and green part of negi. If you care about the presentation of this dish, now is a good time to place each ingredient and fish out the chicken pieces and place on top of udon noodles.

5. Increase the heat to medium, cover with the lid, and cook for 5 minutes. When boiling, turn the heat down to simmer. Once in a while, make sure to check udon or other ingredients are not stuck on the bottom of the pot, by inserting cooking chopsticks. Skim off the fat and scum with a fine mesh skimmer.

6. Add 1 Tbsp miso in the soup. Be careful not to drop the chunk of miso. Use a ladle as a "mixing bowl" so you won't lose the miso.

7. Add kamaboko fish cakes (where it could have a nice color) and carefully drop the eggs in the middle. From this point, you do not want to cover with the lid (egg yolk will have a thin white coating when you cover). Cook for 2-3 minutes.

8. Serve the pot at the table along with individual bowls. Serve in the bowl and sprinkle Shichimi Togarashi for a bit of spicy kick.

Japanese Curry Roux

Japanese Chicken Curry

Prep Time 30 mins

Cook Time 1 hr

Total Time 1 hr 30 mins

Delicious Japanese chicken curry recipe for a weeknight dinner! Tender pieces of chicken, carrots and potatoes cooked in a rich savory curry sauce, this Japanese version of curry is a must-keep for your family meal.

Servings: 6

INGREDIENTS

1.2 lb boneless skinless chicken thighs (544 g or beef, pork, seafood, tofu, or more vegetables)

kosher/sea salt (I use Diamond Crystal; Use half for table salt)

freshly ground black pepper

2 carrots

2 onions

1-2 potatoes

½ Tbsp ginger (grated)

2 cloves garlic

1 ½ Tbsp neutral-flavored oil (vegetable, canola, etc)

4 cups chicken stock/broth (960 ml; OR water OR half stock & half water)

1 apple (I used Fuji apple)

1 Tbsp honey

2 tsp kosher/sea salt (I use Diamond Crystal; Use half for table salt)

1 box Japanese curry roux (7 oz or 200 g) (or use my homemade curry roux recipe)

1 ½ Tbsp soy sauce

1 Tbsp ketchup

Toppings:

soft/hard-boiled egg

Fukujinzuke (red pickled daikon)

INSTRUCTIONS

1. Gather all the ingredients.
2. Discard the extra fat from the chicken and cut it into bite size pieces. Season with a little bit of salt and pepper.
3. Peel and cut the carrot in rolling wedges (Rangiri) and cut the onions in wedges.
4. Cut the potatoes into 1.5 inch pieces and soak in water for 15 minutes to remove excess starch.
5. Grate the ginger and crush the garlic.

6. Heat the oil in a large pot over medium heat and sauté the onions until they become translucent.

7. Add the ginger and garlic.

8. Add the chicken and cook until the chicken changes color.

9. Add the carrot and mix.

10. Add the chicken broth (or water).

11. Bring the stock to boil and skim the scrum and fat from the surface of the stock.

12. Peel the apple and coarsely grate it.

13. Add the honey and salt and simmer uncovered for 20 minutes, stirring occasionally.

14. Add the potatoes and cook for 15 minutes, or until the potatoes are tender, and turn off the heat. Meanwhile you can make homemade curry roux.

15. When the potatoes are ready, add the curry. If you use the store-bought curry roux, put 1-2 blocks of roux in a ladle and slowly let it dissolve with spoon or chopsticks. Continue with the rest of blocks.

16. If you are using homemade curry roux, add a ladleful or two of cooking liquid from the stock and mix into the curry paste. Add more cooking liquid if necessary and mix well until it's smooth.

17. Add the roux paste back into the stock in the large pot

and stir to combine.

18.   Add soy sauce and ketchup. Simmer uncovered on low heat, stirring occasionally, until the curry becomes thick.

19.   Serve the curry with Japanese rice on the side and garnish with soft boiled egg and Fukujinzuke. You can store the curry in the refrigerator up to 2-3 days and in the freezer for 1 month. Potatoes will change the texture so you can take them out before freezing.

Curry Doria (Rice Gratin)

Prep Time 10 mins

Cook Time 30 mins

Total Time 40 mins

Curry Doria is Japanese rice gratin topped with flavorful curry meat sauce and cheese and baked into perfection in a casserole. It screams comfort food!

Servings: 4

INGREDIENTS

3 rice cooker cups uncooked Japanese short-grain rice

½ onion

1 celery stalk

1 carrot

2 cloves garlic

1 Tbsp extra virgin olive oil

1 bay leaf

6 oz ground beef (170 g)

6 oz ground pork (170 g)

kosher/sea salt (I use Diamond Crystal; Use half for table salt)

freshly ground black pepper

1 Tbsp curry powder

1 ½ cups chicken/vegetable stock (360 ml)

2 Tbsp Tonkatsu sauce (Homemade Tonkatsu Sauce recipe)

2 Tbsp ketchup

2 Tbsp unsalted butter (separated)

½ cup Mozzarella cheese (120 ml; You can use other cheese like Parmesan.)

½ cup Romano cheese (120 ml; You can use other cheese like Parmesan.)

2 Tbsp panko (Japanese breadcrumbs)

Parsley (for garnish)

INSTRUCTIONS

1. Gather all the ingredients. Start cooking rice. See How To Cook Rice (rice cooker or stovetop) for reference. You will also need 2 medium-size baking dishes or 1 large baking dish.
2. Mince the onion, celery, and carrot into small pieces.
3. Heat olive oil over medium heat and add crushed (or minced) garlic and a bay leaf (if you tear in half, the fragrance will come out faster).

4. Saute minced onion and celery over medium high heat until they are almost translucent.

5. Add carrot and cook until tender.

6. Add the meat and break it up, stirring occasionally. Cook until the meat is no longer pink.

7. Season with salt and pepper.

8. Add 1 Tbsp curry powder and 1 ½ cup chicken/vegetable broth. If the liquid doesn't cover the ingredients, you will need to add more broth or water.

9. Cover with the lid and bring to a boil. Once boiling, uncover and skim off the foam, fat, scum off from the liquid. It's important to get rid of them so that you can achieve a nice and clean soup. Reduce the heat to medium low and cook for 5 minutes.

10. Add 2 Tbsp Tonkatsu sauce, 2 Tbsp ketchup, and 1 Tbsp butter. The meat mixture should be a bit on saltier side than bland taste. You will be eating this dish with rice, so make sure it's well seasoned. Cook and reduce the sauce until you see the bottom of the pan, about 10 minutes, and turn off the heat.

11. Use the other 1 Tbsp butter to grease the sides and bottom of the baking dish(es). Place the steamed rice in the baking dish.

12. Place the meat mixture (and sauce, if you like) on top of

the rice. Then sprinkle both kinds of cheese. Finally sprinkle panko on top to add crispy texture.

13.   Pre-heat the oven on broil for 5 minutes. Broil for 2-3 minutes until the cheese has melted and you see nice char on top. If you don't have a broil setting, you can simply bake it until the top is golden brown. Everything is already cooked, so all you need to do is melt the cheese.

14.   Sprinkle fresh parsley on top and serve immediately.

Pasta

Creamy Mushroom & Bacon Pasta

Prep Time 5 mins

Cook Time 25 mins

Total Time 30 mins

Creamy Mushroom and Bacon Pasta with a Japanese twist! A dash of soy sauce is the secret ingredient that gives nice umami and savoriness to the dish.

Servings: 2

INGREDIENTS

4 slices bacon (⅓ lb)

½ package shimeji mushrooms (60 g; or use any other mushrooms)

4 cremini mushrooms (52 g; you can also use button mushrooms)

4 shiitake mushrooms (52 g; or use any other mushrooms))

1 ½ Tbsp extra virgin olive oil

2 cloves garlic

For the pasta

8 oz pasta (spaghetti, linguine, or fettuccine; 4 oz/113 g per person)

4 quarts water (4 L)

1 ½ Tbsp kosher/sea salt (I use Diamond Crystal; Use half for table salt)

For the creamy sauce

1 Tbsp unsalted butter

freshly ground black pepper

2 Tbsp all-purpose flour (plain flour) (20 g)

1 cup milk (240 ml)

⅓ cup heavy (whipping) cream (80 ml)

1 Tbsp soy sauce

⅛ tsp kosher/sea salt (I use Diamond Crystal; Use half for table salt)

To Garnish

Parsley

INSTRUCTIONS

1. Gather all the ingredients.
2. Add 1 ½ Tbsp salt in 4 quarts (4L) of water and bring it to a boil for cooking spaghetti. Meanwhile, prepare the rest of the ingredients. Once water is boiling, add spaghetti and cook according to package instructions. Tip 1: Stop cooking 1

minute earlier as you will continue to cook pasta in the frying pan. Tip 2: Before draining the pasta, reserve ½ cup (120 ml) pasta cooking water. Drain well and set aside.

3. Cut the bacon slices into ½ inch (1.25 cm) pieces.

4. Cut the bottom of the mushrooms and slice them. Cut the bottom end of shimeji mushrooms.

5. Remove the stem of shiitake mushrooms and slice them.

6. In a large frying pan, heat 1 ½ Tbsp olive oil on medium heat. Note: if you use a non-stick frying pan, you can skip the oil.

7. Once the oil is hot, add the bacon and sauté.

8. Once the bacon fat renders, crush 2 cloves garlic and add into the pan.

9. Add all the mushrooms and saute together. Add 1 Tbsp butter and freshly ground black pepper.

10.   Add the flour and make sure to keep stirring so the flour doesn't stick at the bottom of the pan.

11.   Stir in 1 cup milk, ⅓ cup heavy cream, and 1 Tbsp soy sauce. Continue scraping off the bottom of the pan. Flour will thicken the sauce.

12.   Taste the sauce and add salt and freshly ground black pepper to taste if necessary. If the sauce is too thick, you can add ¼ cup of pasta cooking water (after that, add a tablespoon one at a time) to dilute the sauce. Tip: You want to make sure it

tastes a bit stronger than you want the final dish to be (because you will add spaghetti).

13. Add cooked spaghetti in the frying pan, or alternatively, you can pour the sauce over the spaghetti on a serving plate. Using the pair of tongs, coat the spaghetti with the sauce.

14. If you like, add freshly ground black pepper. Serve and garnish with parsley.

Japanese Pasta with Shrimp and Asparagus

Prep Time 10 mins

Cook Time 20 mins

Total Time 30 mins

Seasoned with soy sauce and flavorful dashi broth, this Japanese-style Pasta with Shrimp and Asparagus is incredibly delicious and ready in less than 30 minutes! It's also gluten-free!

Servings: 2

INGREDIENTS

¼ red onion (2.5 oz, 70 g)

2 cloves garlic

6 oz asparagus (6 oz, 170 g)

10 large prawn (peeled and deveined; 9 oz, 260 g)

kosher/sea salt (I use Diamond Crystal; Use half for table salt)

freshly ground black pepper

1 Tbsp extra virgin olive oil

1 ½-2 Tbsp unsalted butter

1-2 dried red chili pepper (seeds removed; optional)

¼-⅓ cup dashi (60-80 ml)

1 Tbsp gluten free soy sauce

crushed red peppers (red pepper flakes) (optional)

8 oz gluten free pasta (4 oz or 113 g per person; I used linguini)

INSTRUCTIONS

1. Gather all the ingredients and bring a big pot of water to boil.

2. Meanwhile cut red onion and garlic cloves into thin slices.

3. Cut asparagus diagonally and separate spears and stalks, we will sauté asparagus stalks first as they take longer to cook.

4. Sprinkle kosher salt and freshly ground black pepper on prawn. If your prawn is not peeled or deveined, you can check my tutorial for instructions.

5. Once the pasta water is boiling, for 4QT (16 cups or 3.8L) add 2 Tbsp salt. As we will cook the pasta a little longer after draining, cook it 1 minute less than the directions on the package.

6. Heat 1 Tbsp olive oil in a large skillet over medium heat. When it's hot, add prawn and cook until the bottom side is nicely browned, about 2-3 minutes. Don't touch the shrimp until it releases itself from the skillet. Once it has nice char on one side, you can easily flip.

7. When the one side of the shrimp is nicely browned, flip and cook the other side for 2-3 minutes. Once the shrimp are nicely golden brown, transfer to a plate and set aside.

8. Lower the heat to medium low, add the butter and swirl around.

9. Add the red onion and garlic slices and sauté for 1 minute. If you like spicy pasta, add chili pepper now. Increase the heat to medium and add the stalks of asparagus. Sauté for about 3 minutes, until asparagus stalks become tender.

10. Then add the spears of asparagus and cook for another 1-2 minutes, until the asparagus are tender but still nice and crisp.

11. Add the prawn back in to the skillet and increase the heat to medium high heat. Add dashi.

12. Add gluten free soy sauce and adjust based on your preference.

13. Add the cooked pasta and toss to combine with the ingredients. If you like, sprinkle freshly ground black pepper. Serve immediately. Optionally, you can garnish with chili pepper flake.

Tofu

Tofu Pizza

Prep Time 15 mins

Cook Time 15 mins

Total Time 30 mins

Instead of pizza dough, this Japanese version of Tofu Pizza uses crispy pan-fried tofu as the 'dough' and topped with melted mozzarella cheese, mushrooms, tomato slices and basil leaves for a delicious tofu dish.

Servings: 2

INGREDIENTS

1 block firm tofu

3 slices ham (Skip for vegan/vegetarian)

2 mushrooms

1 tomato

1/4 cup potato starch/cornstarch (You can substitute it with flour)

½ tsp kosher/sea salt (I use Diamond Crystal; Use half for table salt)

freshly ground black pepper

2-3 Tbsp ketchup

2-4 leaves basil

1 cup mozzarella cheese

Parsley (for garnish, optional)

INSTRUCTIONS

1. Gather all the ingredients.

2. Slice the tofu into halves and wrap with paper towel. Place a plate and a heavy object on top of the tofu and set aside for 15 minutes. This process will help tofu drain faster.

3. Slice the ham into thin strips.

4. Thinly slice the mushrooms and the tomato.

5. Season the flour with ½ tsp. salt and freshly ground black pepper and mix well. Coat all sides of tofu with potato starch or flour. This step helps tofu retain the moisture.

6. Heat oil over medium high heat in an oven-safe skillet (or regular non-stick frying pan). Cook the tofu until the bottom is crispy and golden brown. Flip and brown the other side. If your frying pan is not oven safe, transfer the tofu to a baking dish lined with parchment paper later on.

7. Spread ketchup on top and place a slice of tomato and basil.

8. Put the sliced ham and mushrooms on top.

9. Sprinkle some cheese. You can place the pan in the oven and broil for 5-7 minutes, until the cheese has nicely melted. Serve immediately.

Mapo Tofu

Prep Time 10 mins

Cook Time 15 mins

Total Time 25 mins

The Japanese-style Mapo Tofu (Mabo Dofu) is incredibly flavorful but less spicy than the Sichuan-style. A delicious meal ready in 30 minutes that even children can enjoy!

Servings: 4

INGREDIENTS

2 cloves garlic

1 inch ginger (2.5 cm)

2 green onions/scallions

14 oz silken/soft tofu (396 g)

1 Tbsp neutral-flavored oil (vegetable, canola, etc)

½ lb ground pork (227 g; or any other meat/veggies of your choice)

Seasonings

2 ½ Tbsp Doubanjiang (spicy chili bean sauce/broad bean paste) I use 1 ½ Tbsp Doubanjiang (non-spicy) and 1 Tbsp Ladoubanjigang (spicy). You can buy the non-spicy one from this shop online.

2 Tbsp mirin

1 Tbsp miso

1 Tbsp oyster sauce

½ Tbsp soy sauce

1 tsp sesame oil (roasted)

1 tsp potato starch/cornstarch

4 Tbsp water

INSTRUCTIONS

1. Gather all the ingredients.
2. Combine all the ingredients for Seasonings (2 ½ Tbsp Chili Bean Sauce and/or Broad Bean Paste, 2 Tbsp mirin, 1 Tbsp miso, 1 Tbsp. oyster sauce, ½ Tbsp soy sauce, 1 tsp sesame oil, 1 tsp corn starch, 4 Tbsp water) in a bowl and mix well together.
3. Mince the garlic cloves and ginger finely.
4. Cut the green onions into small pieces. Drain the tofu and cut into about 1 inch (2.5 cm) cubes.
5. In a large frying pan, heat vegetable oil on medium heat and saute garlic and ginger. Make sure you don't burn them. Once they are fragrant, add the ground pork and break it up with a spatula or wooden spoon.
6. When the meat is no longer pink, add the Seasoning mixture and stir thoroughly.
7. Once the sauce is back to boiling, add the tofu and gently coat the tofu with the sauce. Stir frequently, without mashing up the tofu, until it is heated through. Add the green onions and mix just before taking the pan off the heat. Serve immediately.

49

Flour

Homemade Gyoza Wrappers

Prep Time 1 hr 15 mins

Total Time 1 hr 45 mins

Have you tried making gyoza wrappers from scratch? All you need is salt, water, and flour! It's that easy. You can either follow the written recipe or watch the cooking video for visual instructions. And enjoy this fun, rewarding process!

Servings: 38 to 42 thin, 3-inch wrappers (using all the dough)

2 cups all-purpose flour (plain flour) (240 g; or 120 g bread flour + 120 g cake flour; See Notes)

½ tsp kosher/sea salt (I use Diamond Crystal; Use half for table salt)

½ cup water (Just boiled, should be around 120-150 ml, plus more if necessary; As different brands of flour will absorb water differently, please adjust the amount of water if necessary.)

potato starch/cornstarch (for dusting)

INSTRUCTIONS

1. Gather all the ingredients.
2. Before you start, you need to accurately measure flour. If you don't have a kitchen scale (I highly recommend getting one like this), stir the flour in the bowl, scoop it up with a spoon, sprinkle into the 1-cup measuring cup, and level off the top. Put the flour into a medium bowl. The amount of flour should be close to standard 4.25 oz (120 g) per cup.
3. Sift the flour into a large bowl.
4. Add salt to just-boiled water and mix until completely

dissolved.

5. Add the just-boiled water into the flour little by little, stirring with a rubber spatula. You will eventually need to use your hands to form the dough into a ball. If the flour is still separated, add ½ Tbsp water at a time till you can form the texture into a ball.

6. Transfer the dough to the work surface and knead the dough for 10 minutes.

7. After 10 minutes, the texture of the dough will be much smoother. Cut the dough in half.

8. Shape each half into a long log, about 1½ inches in diameter (it doesn't have to be perfect if you're going to use a cookie cutter later). Wrap each log with plastic wrap. Let it sit for 30 minutes.

9. Unwrap the dough. Sprinkle a little potato starch on the work surface and cut each log crosswise into about 12 pieces (may vary depending on the log length and width). Since we'll be using a cookie cutter, don't worry if each piece of dough has slightly different size.

10.   Cover the dough with damp kitchen towel at all time to prevent from drying.

11.   For each piece of dough into a ball shape.

12.   Press the ball onto the work surface.

13.   Using a rolling pin, roll out the dough, but DO NOT roll

out (flatten) the TOP and BOTTOM edge. This is a trick to make a nice round shape.

14.   Rotate the dough 90 degrees and repeat rolling the dough to make a nice round shape. Try to roll out the dough to a thin circle. If the dough is hard to roll out or shrinks back, let the dough rest a bit to relax the gluten.

15.   [Optional] If you want a perfectly round shape for your wrappers, press down the 3-inch (8 cm) cookie cutter and remove excess dough. If the dough rolls back, leave it for a few seconds, and cut out. Cover the scraps with the damp towel. Later combine all the scraps as long as they still squish together and haven't dried out too much. Re-roll the scraps and repeat the process.

16.   Sprinkle each wrapper with potato starch and stack the gyoza wrappers. Make sure to the wrappers covered with damp kitchen towel. Once all the dough is used, wrap the gyoza wrappers with plastic wrap and freeze or refrigerate until you're ready to use. You can keep gyoza wrappers for about 3-4 days in the refrigerator and up to a month in freezer. Defrost in the refrigerator prior to use.

Okonomiyaki

Prep Time 30 mins

Cook Time 30 mins

Total Time 2 hrs

Hailing from Osaka, Okonomiyaki is a delicious Japanese savory pancake made with flour, eggs, cabbage, and protein, and topped with a variety of condiments.

Servings: 4

INGREDIENTS

1 cup all-purpose flour (plain flour) (120 g)

¼ tsp kosher/sea salt (I use Diamond Crystal; Use half for table salt)

¼ tsp sugar

¼ tsp baking powder

2-3 inch Nagaimo/Yamaimo (5-8 cm, 160 g, 5.6 oz)

¾ cup dashi (180 ml; You can make Dashi or use ¾ cup water + 1 tsp dashi powder. For vegetarian, use Kombu Dashi.)

1 large cabbage head (1.6 lb or 740 g)

½ lb sliced pork belly (227 g; You can thinly slice the pork belly if your pork belly is a slab. You can sub with shrimp or squid. For vegetarian, skip and use mushroom.)

4 large eggs

½ cup Tenkasu/Agedama (tempura scraps) (8 Tbsp)

¼ cup pickled red ginger (beni shoga or kizami beni shoga) (4 Tbsp)

neutral-flavored oil (vegetable, canola, etc)

Quick Okonomiyaki Sauce

1 ½ Tbsp sugar

2 Tbsp oyster sauce

4 Tbsp ketchup

3 ½ Tbsp Worcestershire sauce

Toppings

Okonomi sauce

Japanese mayonnaise

Katsuobushi (dried bonito flakes) (Skip for vegetarian)

Aonori (dried green seaweed)

Green onions/scallions

pickled red ginger (beni shoga or kizami beni shoga)

INSTRUCTIONS

Gather all the ingredients.

To Prepare Okonomiyaki Batter

1. In a large bowl, combine 1 cup (120 g) all-purpose flour, ¼ tsp salt, ¼ tsp sugar, and ¼ tsp baking powder and mix all together.

2. Peel and grate nagaimo in a small bowl. It can get itchy, so

work quickly and rinse your hand right after. Nagaimo is very slimy and slippery, so make sure you have a good grip if you wear a glove.

3. Add the grated nagaimo and dashi in the bowl.

4. Mix all together till combined. Cover the bowl with plastic wrap and let it rest in the refrigerator for at least one hour.

To Make Okonomiyaki Sauce

1. Meanwhile, gather all the ingredients for Okonomiyaki Sauce.

2. Okonomiyaki Sauce Ingredients

3. Combine 1 ½ Tbsp sugar, 2 Tbsp oyster sauce, 4 Tbsp ketchup, and 3 ½ Tbsp Worcestershire sauce in a small bowl. Mix all together until sugar is completely dissolved.

To Prepare Okonomiyaki

1. Remove the core of the cabbage and mince it. Set aside to let the moisture evaporate so it won't dilute the batter.

2. Cut the pork belly slices in half and set aside.

3. Take out the batter from the refrigerator and add 4 large eggs, ½ cup (8 Tbsp) tempura scraps (Tenkasu/Agedama), and ¼ cup (4 Tbsp) pickled red ginger (Kizami Beni Shoga) in the bowl. Mix well until well-combined.

4. Add chopped cabbage to the batter ⅓ at a time. Mix well

before adding the rest.

To Grill Okonomiyaki

1. In a large pan, heat vegetable oil on medium heat. When the frying pan is hot (400 F or 200 °C), spread the batter in a circle on the pan. We like thicker okonomiyaki (final thickness is ¾ inches or 2 cm). If you're new to making okonomiyaki, make a smaller and thinner size so it's easier to flip.

2. Place 2-3 sliced pork belly on top of Okonomiyaki and cook covered for 5 minutes.

3. When the bottom side is nicely browned, flip over.

4. Gently press the okonomiyaki to fix the shape and keep it together. Cover and cook for another 5 minutes.

5. Flip over one last time and cook uncovered for 2 minutes. If you're going to cook next batch, transfer to a plate.

To Serve

1. Here are the ingredients for toppings. Apply okonomiyaki sauce with brush, add Japanese mayonnaise in zigzagging lines (optional), and sprinkle dried bonito flakes (katsuobushi). You can also put dried green seaweed (aonori), chopped green onions, and pickled red ginger on top for garnish. Please see

the video for this step.

2. To Store

3. Okonomiyaki freezes well. Once it cools down (no sauce or toppings), wrap each okonomiyaki in aluminum foil and put it in a freezer bag. When you want to eat it, defrost first and put it in a toaster oven or oven to heat it up. It's a great quick meal!

To Cook Several Okonomiyaki At Once

1. If you have a Japanese griddle with a lid (We call it "Hot Plate"), you can cook several okonomiyaki at once! Otherwise, I recommend cooking two okonomiyaki (each in one frying pan) at a time.

Fluffy Japanese Souffle Pancakes

Prep Time 15 mins

Cook Time 15 mins chilling time 15 mins

Total Time 45 mins

These Fluffy Japanese Souffle Pancakes are like eating cottony clouds, but even better with homemade whipped cream and fresh berries!

Servings: 3 pancakes (1 serving)

INGREDIENTS

2 large eggs

1 ½ Tbsp whole milk (22 g)

¼ tsp pure vanilla extract

¼ cup cake flour (30 g; If you're using a cup measurement, please follow this method to measure. Otherwise, the amount of flour tends to be more than you need. You can make your Homemade Cake Flour.)

½ tsp baking powder (2 g)

2 Tbsp sugar (25 g)

1 Tbsp neutral-flavored oil (vegetable, canola, etc) (for greasing the pan)

2 Tbsp water (for steaming)

Fresh Whipped Cream (optional)

½ cup heavy (whipping) cream (120 ml)

1 ½ Tbsp sugar (20 g)

Toppings

1 Tbsp confectioners' sugar/powder sugar

Fresh berries

maple syrup

INSTRUCTIONS

2. Gather all the ingredients. You will also need a 12-inch non-stick frying pan (large enough to cook 3 pancakes at the same time) with a lid.

3. Separate egg whites and egg yolks into two different bowls. Put the bowl with egg whites in the freezer for 15 minutes. Why do we freeze egg whites? Please read 3 Tips to Make Perfect Meringue (Egg Whites) in this post.

4. In the meantime, add milk and vanilla to the egg yolks and whisk until thick and frothy.

5. Sift the cake flour and baking powder into the bowl.

6. Whisk to combine thoroughly (but do not over-mix). Set aside.

7. After 15 minutes, take out the bowl with egg whites from the

freezer. The egg whites should be half frozen. Now start beating egg whites.

8. When the egg whites turn frothy and pale white, gradually add in sugar (roughly ⅓ at a time). Continue to whip the egg whites.

9. The egg whites will become glossier and firmer. Stop beating when you lift up the hand mixer and the egg whites stand right up with stiff peaks slightly bending over.

10. Heat the large non-stick frying pan to 300 °F (150 °C) over the lowest heat. Brush with cooking oil and lightly remove any visible oil (otherwise the pancakes will have a spotty pattern). Keep the heat on while you combine egg whites and egg yolk mixture.

11. Take ⅓ of egg whites and add to the egg yolk mixture. Whisk together (don't worry too much about breaking air bubbles at this step).

12. Next, take half of the egg whites and add to the egg yolk mixture. Using a whisk, gently fold in without breaking the air bubbles in the egg whites. Why do we use a whisk instead of a silicone spatula? Please read 3 Tips to Make Perfect Meringue (Egg Whites) in this post.

13. Now transfer the egg yolk mixture into egg whites. Carefully fold in two mixtures together without breaking the air bubbles. Make sure to gently mix the batter thoroughly!

14. For my stove and frying pan, I kept 300 °F (150 °C) all times on low heat. Remember each pancake gets roughly 4 scoops of batter, so that's a total of 12 scoops for 3 pancakes. Now, scoop the batter and place on the frying pan. My recommendation is to use a small ladle (or a serving spoon that's bigger than a regular spoon - probably 2-3 Tbsp) and make a tall pancake. Next, stack one more scoop to the first pancake. Then move on to the next two pancakes giving each 2 small scoops.

15. By the time all 3 pancakes have 2 scoops, the surface of the batter is slightly dry already, so you can stack one more scoop on top, keeping it up high. In the bowl, you should still have roughly 3 scoops left (if you have slightly more, that's okay).

16. Set timer for 6-7 minutes, add 1 Tbsp water in 3 empty spaces inside the pan and cover with the lid. Water keeps the pancake moist. Please note: the suggested time is just a guideline and it's based on the stove and frying pan that I'm using.

17. After 2 minutes passed, open the lid, and add one more scoop for each pancake (or more scoops if you have more batter). Make sure to stack high, not wide. If the water has evaporated, add a little bit more. Cover with lid and cook.

18. After 6-7 minutes passed, using the offset spatula, lift the pancake VERY GENTLY. If you feel the pancake is stuck, don't touch until they firm up a little. If you force it, the pancake will crack in the middle. When the pancake is ready, you can easily move the pancake.

19. Here is another set of images to show the process. Slightly pull the pancake to create an empty space and gently flip over with "rolling over" motion.

20. Add water in empty spaces and set a timer for 4 to 5 minutes to cook the other side on the lowest heat.

21. Once they are nicely browned, transfer the pancakes to your serving plates.

22. Place fresh cream on the pancakes and top with berries. Dust the pancake with confectioners' sugar and drizzle with maple syrup. Enjoy!

Fresh Whipped Cream

1. Prepare an ice bath by putting ice cubes and water in a large bowl and placing a clean and dry mixing bowl over. Add heavy cream and sugar to keep cool.

2. Whisk on high speed until medium to firm peaks form (should not be runny, but soft and fluffy firm whipped cream). Keep it chilled until you're ready to serve the pancakes.

RECIPE NOTES

How to Prevent Your Souffle Pancakes from Collapsing:

- Souffle pancakes can be tricky to make, so make sure to read my tips in the post thoroughly.

- Beat your egg whites correctly. Any under or overbeating will cause the pancakes to deflate after cooking.

- Cook over low heat, and make sure the inside of the pancakes are properly cooked through.

Printed in Great Britain
by Amazon